LEE MEYER

Real Estate Investing is a Team Sport

A Diverse and Skilled Team Will Get You the Win

Copyright © 2024 by Lee Meyer

All rights reserved. No part of this publication may be reproduced, stored or transmitted in any form or by any means, electronic, mechanical, photocopying, recording, scanning, or otherwise without written permission from the publisher. It is illegal to copy this book, post it to a website, or distribute it by any other means without permission.

Designations used by companies to distinguish their products are often claimed as trademarks. All brand names and product names used in this book and on its cover are trade names, service marks, trademarks and registered trademarks of their respective owners. The publishers and the book are not associated with any product or vendor mentioned in this book. None of the companies referenced within the book have endorsed the book.

First edition

This book was professionally typeset on Reedsy. Find out more at reedsy.com

Contents

Introduction	vi
Real Estate Agents	1
Training and Experience	3
Timely Expertise	3
Pricing and Market Value	4
Contracts and Details	4
More Than a Sign in the Yard	5
Negotiating and Closing the Deal	5
Building Relationships	5
Compensation and Consulting	6
Money!	7
To Pay Cash or Not to Pay Cash?	8
Mortgages: Finding the Right Fit	9
Contractors	11
Building Your Dream Team	12
Rule #1: Always Be There When the Contractor Starts Work	14
Insurance	15
Tailoring Your Coverage to Your Investment	16
Navigating High-Risk Areas	17
Real Estate Attorney and/or Title Company	18
The Role of the Real Estate Attorney	19
The Importance of a Title Company	20
State-by-State Variations	20
Choosing the Right Professionals for Your Team	21

Property Manager	22
The Case for Professional Property Management	23
Leveraging Expertise in Tenant Relations	24
Financial and Legal Benefits	24
Personal Safety and Security	25
Bookkeeper/CPA	26
Taxes!	27
Keeping Your Finances in Order	28
Legal Compliance and Audits	28
Choosing the Right CPA	29
Property Inspector	30
The Role of a Property Inspector	31
Decision-Making Insights	31
Choosing the Right Inspector	32
The Importance of Regular Inspections	32
House Cleaning Team	34
The Importance of Make-Ready Cleaning	35
Cleaning Services for Short-Term Rentals	35
Choosing a Cleaning Service	36
Long-Term Benefits	36
Networking Groups	38
The Value of Real Estate Networking Groups	39
Finding the Right Networking Group	40
Making the Most of Networking Groups	41
Conclusion	42
Building a Championship Team	43
Lessons from the Field	44
Wrapping Up	44
Resources	46

Introduction

Investing in real estate is often seen as a straightforward path to financial freedom, but in reality, it demands a combination of knowledge, money, and time. The good news? You don't have to have all the answers—or resources—right from the start. The first step is building your knowledge base. Dive into books, attend networking meetings, and listen closely to the wisdom shared by guest speakers. Set aside a budget specifically for coffee, lunch, or happy hour meetings where you can have one-on-one conversations with experienced investors. These discussions are invaluable; they allow you to tap into the collective knowledge of those who've walked the path before you.

As you soak up information and gain insight, you'll start to see which type of real estate investing aligns with your goals and resources. Whether it's flipping single-family homes, holding properties for rental income, partnering in syndications, or providing funds for private lending, there's a strategy that fits your situation. But here's the essential truth: no matter which path you choose, there simply aren't enough hours in the day for one person to do everything. Success in real estate isn't a solo endeavor—it's a team sport.

This is where the power of a well-rounded team comes into play. By leveraging the skills and expertise of others, you can amplify your efforts and achieve far more than you ever could alone. Whether it's a real estate agent with local market knowledge, a contractor with the skills to transform a property, or a property manager who keeps everything running smoothly, building a team isn't just a smart move—it's essential.

So, as you start to play this game, remember: the strength of your team will directly impact the level of your success. Let's get started.

Real Estate Agents

When it comes to building a successful real estate investment strategy, one of your most valuable assets will be a knowledgeable and experienced real estate agent. While it might be tempting to go it alone or lean on minimal resources, partnering with the right agent can significantly increase your chances of success. Think of them as your on-the-ground strategist, armed with insights that can make or break a deal.

A licensed real estate agent, especially one who's also an investor, brings more to the table than just the ability to list and sell properties. These agents have a comprehensive playbook that goes beyond the basics, offering you deeper insights into the market, access to exclusive opportunities, and a strategic advantage that's hard to match. When you're navigating the competitive playing field of real estate investing, this expertise is invaluable.

One of the key benefits of working with a real estate agent is the productivity boost they provide. They don't just find properties—they find the right properties. Whether you're investing in your local area or exploring opportunities out of state, an agent with local expertise can help you navigate unfamiliar markets with confidence. For example, if you're based in California but have your eye on the booming real estate market in Texas, establishing a relationship with an agent or broker in Texas is a game-changer. They serve as your boots on the ground, providing you with the data, insights, and local knowledge that can make all the difference.

It's important to understand that the titles and roles of agents and brokers can vary by state. In some places, everyone is referred to as a broker, while in others, the distinction between agent and broker depends on their level of education, training, and testing. Many have also joined the National Association of Realtors®, the largest trade group in the country, which holds its members to a higher ethical standard through the Realtor® Code of Ethics. Whether they're

Realtors® or not, all licensed agents and brokers have a fiduciary responsibility to their clients, meaning they're legally obligated to act in your best interest. This level of commitment ensures that by adding one or more of these professionals to your team, you're tapping into a wealth of skills and knowledge that can propel your investing career forward.

But what exactly should you look for in a real estate agent? And how do you find one with the expertise you need? It all starts with understanding the value they bring to the table.

Training and Experience

The right real estate agent has more than just a license—they have a deep understanding of the entire real estate process, honed through years of experience and additional training. They've seen deals succeed and fail, and they know what it takes to close a deal smoothly. They also bring a network of contacts to the table, from other agents to contractors, inspectors, and more, all of which can be leveraged to your benefit. This breadth of experience and connection is something that only comes with time, and it's one of the biggest reasons to invest in a relationship with a seasoned agent.

Timely Expertise

National housing market headlines can be misleading when it comes to local real estate conditions. What's happening in one region might not apply at all to another, and a good agent knows this. They have access to in-depth, up-to-the-minute data about the specific markets you're interested in, helping you make informed decisions with confidence. They'll help you see past the noise and focus on what really matters: how the market conditions in your target area align with your investment goals.

Pricing and Market Value

You've likely heard the phrase, "You make your money when you buy." It's a mantra in real estate investing, and it underscores the importance of purchasing properties at the right price. The right agent is your secret weapon in this regard. They have access to comprehensive data on comparable sales, property conditions, and potential rental income—all of which are crucial for making smart buying decisions. They can guide you on how to price a property correctly, both when buying and when it's time to sell. Overpricing can lead to increased days on market, which can spook buyers and diminish your negotiating power. A skilled agent will help you avoid these pitfalls by providing a clear, data-driven pricing strategy.

Contracts and Details

Real estate transactions involve a lot of paperwork—contracts, disclosures, and various other documents that can be overwhelming to navigate. While agents can't give legal advice or draft documents unless they're also licensed attorneys, they do have extensive training in managing the transaction process. They know what's required to protect your interests and can help ensure that all the necessary paperwork is completed accurately and on time. This attention to detail minimizes the risk of liability and keeps the transaction moving smoothly towards closing.

More Than a Sign in the Yard

For Sale By Owner (FSBO) is often touted as a way to save on commission fees, but when it comes to selling an investment property for top dollar, FSBO is usually a bad idea. A good listing agent brings strategies, marketing tools, and a network of potential buyers to the table—all of which are critical for attracting offers and closing deals. And because agents only get paid when the deal closes, their marketing efforts don't cost you anything upfront. This investment in your success is what makes hiring an agent a smart move, especially when the goal is to maximize your return on investment.

Negotiating and Closing the Deal

Real estate investing is time-consuming, and juggling all the details can be challenging—especially if you're balancing it with a full-time job. That's where your agent steps in, handling everything from scheduling inspections to referring you to reliable contractors and title companies. They'll keep the ball rolling, ensuring that the transaction stays on track. Additionally, your agent can act as a buffer during negotiations, providing insight into the motivations of the other party and helping you craft a strategy that increases your chances of a successful outcome. This is especially valuable when negotiations get tough, as it often leads to finding a win-win solution that might not have been apparent otherwise.

Building Relationships

Developing relationships with licensed agents in the areas where you want to invest is crucial. Take the time to attend real estate investing meetups and networking events where you can meet agents face-to-face. When you find one who clicks with your style and understands your goals, nurture that relationship. A good agent is not just a service provider—they're a long-term partner in your real estate journey.

Compensation and Consulting

Most real estate agents work on commission, meaning they get paid when a deal closes. However, if you're relying on your agent for extensive work outside of specific transactions—like detailed market analysis or ongoing strategy discussions—consider negotiating a consulting fee. Just as you would pay other professionals on your team for their expertise, compensating your agent fairly for their time and insights helps keep them engaged and motivated. It's an investment in the relationship, and it pays dividends when you're navigating complex deals.

In summary, a real estate agent isn't just a necessary part of your investing team—they're a key player who can significantly impact your success. By leveraging their expertise, connections, and market knowledge, you can streamline your investing process, minimize risks, and maximize your returns. As you move forward in your real estate journey, remember that finding the right agent is a crucial step in winning the game!

Money!

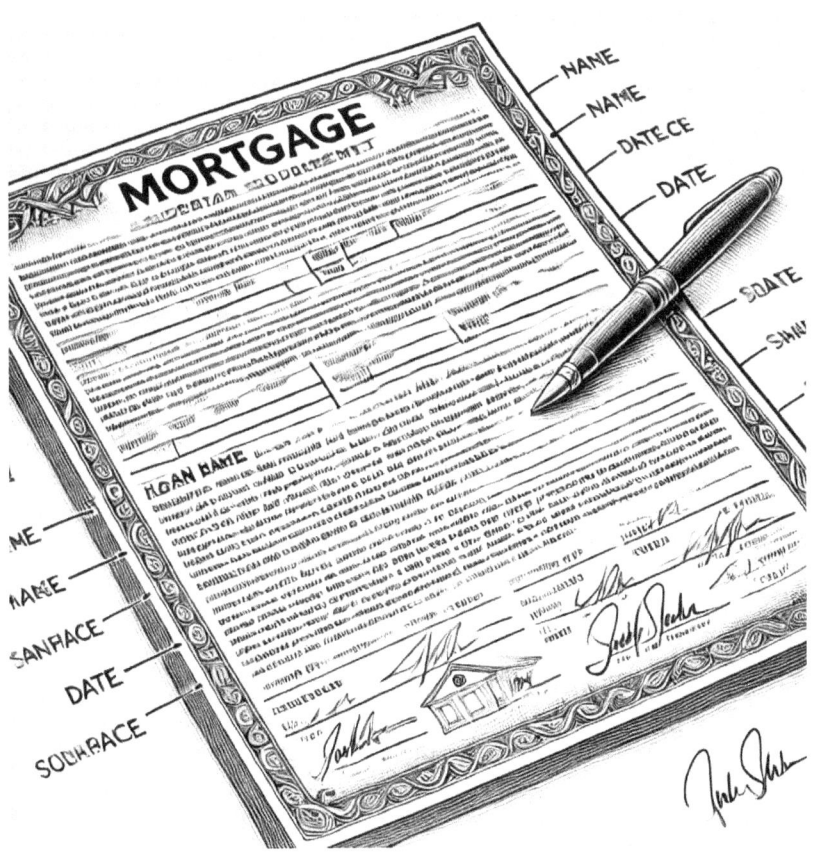

Money ensures that each investment moves downfield towards the goal of financial success in real estate investing. Whether you're flush with cash or just starting out, understanding how to leverage your financial resources is fundamental to building a successful investment portfolio. The choices you make about financing can significantly impact your returns, so it's essential to have a clear strategy that aligns with your goals.

To Pay Cash or Not to Pay Cash?

If you have a substantial bank account or an inheritance burning a hole in your pocket, paying cash for an investment property might seem like a straightforward option. There's a certain appeal to owning a property outright—no mortgage payments, no interest, and potentially less risk. But is it the best use of your capital?

Consider this scenario: You have $500,000 in cash. You could use that to buy one house outright, avoiding any debt. Alternatively, you could take that same $500,000 and use it as a 25% down payment on four properties, each valued at $500,000. By doing so, you're leveraging other people's money (OPM) to multiply your investment. With tenants paying rent, which covers your mortgage payments, you're effectively using leverage to grow your portfolio faster.

Leverage is one of the most powerful tools in real estate investing. It allows you to control more assets with less of your own money, potentially increasing your returns. However, leverage also introduces risk. If the market turns, you could find yourself with properties worth less than the debt you owe on them. Therefore, the decision to use leverage should be made carefully, with a thorough understanding of both the rewards and the risks.

Mortgages: Finding the Right Fit

Mortgages come in many shapes and sizes, and choosing the right one for your situation is critical. Traditional mortgages are available from big banks, credit unions, and mortgage brokers. Each option has its own set of benefits and drawbacks.

Mortgage Brokers: These professionals have access to a wide variety of loan products from different lenders. They can shop around on your behalf, potentially finding you better terms than you might get from a single bank. Mortgage brokers can also be more flexible and responsive, which is a significant advantage in a competitive market.

Small Local Banks: Don't overlook the power of local connections. Small local banks are often more community-focused and may offer more personalized service. They understand the local market better and may be willing to offer more favorable terms or be more flexible in their lending criteria, especially if they believe in your investment plan. Establishing a strong banking relationship in the area where you want to invest can be a smart move, providing you with a reliable financial partner who understands your goals.

Hard Money and Private Lending: Quick, but Risky

For investors looking at deals with quick turnaround times, hard money or private lending might be the best option. Unlike traditional mortgages, these loans are often based more on the value of the property and the specifics of the deal than on the borrower's creditworthiness. This can make them an attractive option if you need to move quickly or if your credit history isn't perfect.

However, hard money and private loans come with higher interest rates and fees, reflecting the increased risk for the lender. They're typically short-term, often 12 months or less, which means you need to have a clear and achievable exit strategy from the outset. Whether it's a quick flip, refinancing into a traditional mortgage, or another investment strategy, make sure you have more than one potential exit plan. Market shifts, supply chain disruptions, or unexpected repairs can all derail your timeline, so it's essential to have contingency plans in place.

Evaluating Your Options

When deciding on your financing strategy, it's important to evaluate all the options available to you. Start by assessing your financial situation—how much capital do you have available, and what is your risk tolerance? Then, consider your investment goals—are you looking for long-term appreciation, short-term gains, or a mix of both? The answers to these questions will guide you in choosing the right financing options.

The goal of real estate investing isn't just to acquire properties—it's to create wealth. The right financing strategy will help you maximize your returns while managing your risk. Whether you choose to pay cash, leverage with a traditional mortgage, or opt for hard money loans, the key is to make informed decisions based on a thorough understanding of the pros and cons.

In the world of real estate investing, money isn't just a tool—it's the foundation of your entire strategy. By understanding how to best leverage your financial resources, you can maximize your investments, manage risk, and build a portfolio that delivers strong returns over time.

Contractors

When it comes to real estate investing, the right contractors are like the star players on your team—essential for driving value in your investment properties. Most investment properties involve value-add transactions, where strategic renovations and updates increase the property's market value and boost your returns. Trying to do it all yourself might seem cost-effective, but it's often a false economy. The time you spend swinging a hammer could be better spent finding the next deal, securing financing, or strategizing your exit plan. This is where having a reliable network of skilled contractors can make all the difference.

Building Your Dream Team

Your contractor team should be a well-rounded group of professionals, each bringing their specialized expertise to the table. Here's a breakdown of the key players you'll need:

General Contractor: The general contractor is the quarterback of your renovation team. They manage the overall project, coordinating with all the other contractors and ensuring that everything is done on time and within budget. A good general contractor will have a deep understanding of the renovation process, be well-versed in local building codes, and have a network of trusted subcontractors to call on.

Electrician: Electrical work is one area where you don't want to cut corners. A licensed electrician ensures that all wiring, lighting, and electrical systems meet safety standards and are up to code. Poor electrical work can lead to costly repairs down the road or, worse, create dangerous conditions that could jeopardize the safety of tenants or future buyers.

Plumber: Plumbing issues are a common concern in older properties, and they can be both complex and expensive to fix. A skilled plumber will handle everything from installing new fixtures to repairing leaks and ensuring that the plumbing system is up to modern standards. Proper plumbing is crucial for maintaining property value and avoiding future headaches.

HVAC Company: Heating, ventilation, and air conditioning systems are critical for tenant comfort and energy efficiency. An experienced HVAC contractor will evaluate the existing system, make necessary repairs or upgrades, and ensure that the property meets current energy efficiency standards. This can not only increase the property's value but also make it more appealing to potential buyers or renters.

Landscape and Yard Maintenance: Curb appeal matters. The exterior of your property is the first thing people see, and a well-maintained yard can significantly boost its perceived value. A landscaping company can handle everything from lawn care to more extensive projects like installing walkways, patios, or even outdoor living spaces that enhance the property's appeal.

Foundation Company: Foundation issues can be a deal-breaker for many buyers, so it's crucial to address any problems early on. A reputable foundation company can assess the condition of the foundation, make necessary repairs, and provide a warranty that can reassure potential buyers. Investing in foundation work can prevent costly issues down the road and add significant value to your property. Foundation issues don't have to be scary, they're just a fact of life in some areas.

Rule #1: Always Be There When the Contractor Starts Work

One of the most important lessons you'll learn as a real estate investor is that being present at the start of a project can save you a lot of trouble later on. When you're there in person, you can confirm that the contractor understands the scope of work, discuss any last-minute details, and set expectations. It's also a great time to build rapport and establish clear communication, which is key to ensuring that the project runs smoothly.

Unfortunately, many investors have learned this the hard way—taking a contractor's word at face value, only to find that the work started late, wasn't done as agreed, or encountered unexpected issues that could have been addressed early on. By being present at the beginning, you can head off these problems and keep the project on track.

Remember, the success of your investment often hinges on the quality of the work done by your contractors. Choose them wisely, build strong relationships, and always be there when the work begins. With the right team in place, you'll be well on your way to achieving your real estate investment goals.

Insurance

Insurance for real estate investments isn't as simple as just getting another homeowner's policy like you have on your primary residence. When you're dealing with investment properties, especially those that are vacant, under renovation, or intended for rental, you need specialized coverage to protect your assets. Understanding the nuances of different insurance policies is crucial to safeguarding your investment and ensuring you're not left exposed in the event of damage, liability claims, or other unexpected situations.

Tailoring Your Coverage to Your Investment

When a property is vacant during renovations, a standard homeowner's policy won't cut it. You'll need a vacant property policy, which covers the specific risks associated with unoccupied homes, such as vandalism, theft, or fire. These policies are tailored to the unique vulnerabilities of a property that isn't being lived in and can offer the peace of mind that your investment is protected even when no one is on-site.

If contractors are working on the property, you need to ensure that your insurance covers not just the building itself but also any potential liability issues that could arise from the renovation work. This might include damage caused by the contractors, accidents on-site, or issues related to the work being done. Having this coverage in place before the first hammer falls is essential.

Once tenants move in, the insurance requirements change again. A landlord insurance policy will cover not just the structure of the building but also any liability issues that could arise from renting it out. This could include coverage for legal fees if a tenant sues you, loss of rental income if the property becomes uninhabitable due to a covered event, and more. The type of coverage you need may also vary based on the rental model—long-term leases versus short-term rentals, for instance, often require different types of insurance.

Navigating High-Risk Areas

If your property is in a high-risk area, such as a coastal region prone to flooding or hurricanes, you'll need specialized insurance for these risks. Wind and flood insurance can be expensive, but they are non-negotiable if you want to protect your investment. Not having this coverage could be financially devastating in the event of a natural disaster.

In these situations, your usual insurance provider might not offer the best coverage at a competitive rate. This is where a knowledgeable insurance broker who specializes in real estate investment properties becomes invaluable. A good broker will understand the unique risks associated with investment properties and can guide you toward the right policies that offer the protection you need without breaking the bank.

The right insurance coverage is like a solid defense in a team sport—it might not be the most glamorous part of the game, but it's absolutely essential to winning in the long run. By securing the appropriate policies for each stage of your investment, you ensure that you're protected against the unexpected and can focus on growing your portfolio with confidence.

Real Estate Attorney and/or Title Company

REAL ESTATE ATTORNEY AND/OR TITLE COMPANY

In the world of real estate investing, having the right legal and title experts on your team is crucial to navigating the complexities of transactions, ensuring that your investments are secure, and minimizing the risks that come with property ownership. The terms "Closing," "Escrow," "Title Search," "Commitment for Title Insurance," "Shortages in Area," and "Foreclosure" are just a few of the critical elements that a knowledgeable real estate attorney or title company can help you manage effectively.

The Role of the Real Estate Attorney

Real estate attorneys are specialized legal professionals who understand the intricacies of property law, and they play a vital role in guiding you through the legal aspects of real estate transactions. Whether you're purchasing a single-family home, investing in commercial property, or diving into foreclosure deals, a real estate attorney ensures that every part of your transaction is legally sound. They review contracts, negotiate terms, and handle the closing process, ensuring that your rights are protected and that you understand all the legal obligations and risks involved.

One of the key responsibilities of a real estate attorney is to conduct a thorough review of all documents related to the transaction. This includes the purchase agreement, title documents, mortgage agreements, and any other contracts or disclosures. They also help to resolve any legal issues that may arise, such as disputes over property boundaries, zoning issues, or problems with the title. If you're dealing with more complex transactions, such as those involving foreclosures or short sales, an experienced real estate attorney can be invaluable in navigating the additional legal challenges these situations present.

The Importance of a Title Company

A title company plays an equally important role in ensuring that the property you are purchasing has a clear and marketable title. The title company conducts a title search to identify any potential issues that could affect your ownership, such as liens, unpaid taxes, or disputed property boundaries. They also provide title insurance, which protects you against any future claims or disputes over the property's ownership. This is particularly important in real estate investing, where any legal challenge to your ownership could have significant financial implications.

The title company also manages the escrow process, holding funds, and documents until all conditions of the sale are met. This neutral third party ensures that the buyer and seller fulfill their obligations, providing a layer of security to both parties. When the conditions of the sale are satisfied, the title company disburses the funds and transfers the title to the new owner.

State-by-State Variations

It's important to note that real estate transactions can vary significantly from state to state, so what works in one area might not be applicable in another. For instance, some states require attorneys to be involved in every real estate transaction, while others do not. Additionally, the terminology and processes can differ—what one state calls a "closing" might be known as a "settlement" in another, and the responsibilities of the title company versus the attorney can shift as well.

When investing in properties outside of your home state, it's essential to educate yourself on the specific laws and procedures of that state. Your real estate agent can often be a valuable resource in this area, connecting you with reputable attorneys and title companies who are well-versed in local practices. Additionally, networking with other investors who have experience in that state can provide you with insights and referrals to trusted professionals.

Choosing the Right Professionals for Your Team

It's important to choose a real estate attorney and title company who are experienced in the type of transactions you plan to undertake. A general practice attorney or a title company that primarily handles residential home sales may not have the expertise needed for more complex investment deals. For instance, if you're dealing with foreclosures, short sales, or commercial properties, you'll want a team that has specific experience in those areas.

Don't be afraid to ask potential attorneys and title companies about their experience with real estate investors and the types of transactions you're pursuing. You want to ensure they are not only knowledgeable but also proactive in identifying and solving potential issues before they become problems. The right legal and title team can be the difference between a smooth, successful transaction and one that is fraught with delays, complications, and unexpected costs.

In real estate investing, your attorney and title company are like the referees in a game—ensuring that everything is fair, legal, and above board. By carefully selecting professionals who are experienced, knowledgeable, and well-versed in your specific needs, you can protect your investments and navigate the complexities of real estate transactions with confidence.

Property Manager

Managing a real estate investment effectively can be as crucial as the initial purchase. While some investors choose to handle property management themselves, the complexities and demands of managing properties can often justify the expense of hiring a professional property manager. This chapter explores the roles of property managers and the benefits they bring, especially for investors who are expanding their portfolios or those who simply cannot be on-site regularly.

The Case for Professional Property Management

Many investors start out managing their own properties to save on costs. This can work well for a while, especially when the properties are local and demands are manageable. However, property management can quickly become overwhelming, particularly as your portfolio grows or if your properties are not local. It's also common for issues to arise at the most inopportune times—such as when you're out of town. Having a professional property manager can mitigate these disruptions by ensuring there is always someone available to handle emergencies, perform regular maintenance, and manage tenant relations smoothly.

A professional property manager does more than just handle day-to-day operations; they bring a comprehensive understanding of the local real estate market, including laws and regulations that govern rental properties. This knowledge is invaluable in maintaining compliance with federal Fair Housing laws and local ordinances, which can vary significantly from one area to another. Property managers also handle all aspects of tenant management, from screening and leasing to renewals and evictions, ensuring that these processes are handled professionally and legally.

Leveraging Expertise in Tenant Relations

Effective property management involves thorough tenant screening processes, including credit and criminal background checks, verification of rental history, and employment checks. These steps are critical in securing reliable tenants and minimizing turnover and rental disputes. Professional property managers have access to tools and systems that streamline these checks, ensuring they are done thoroughly and efficiently.

Moreover, property managers are skilled in marketing rental properties. They know the most effective strategies and platforms for advertising vacancies beyond just placing a sign in the yard or posting on Craigslist. This can include listing on high-traffic rental websites, using social media platforms, and leveraging professional networks to find tenants quickly, reducing the time your property remains vacant.

Financial and Legal Benefits

Incorporating the cost of property management in your initial financial calculations gives you a realistic view of your potential returns. While it is an additional expense, the benefits often outweigh the costs. Professional managers can optimize rental income and maintain high occupancy rates, while also ensuring that maintenance issues are addressed promptly and cost-effectively, preserving the value of your investment.

From a legal standpoint, property managers are well-versed in the latest property laws and stay updated on any changes. This expertise is crucial in protecting you from potential lawsuits and financial penalties that could arise from non-compliance with housing regulations.

Personal Safety and Security

Property management also involves personal interactions that can sometimes be risky, such as showing vacant properties or meeting with tenants to resolve disputes. Professional property managers are trained to handle these situations safely and effectively, minimizing your personal risk and ensuring that all interactions are conducted professionally.

The decision to hire a property manager should be weighed against the scale of your investment, your availability, and how hands-on you want to be in managing your properties. While self-managing can work for smaller or local portfolios, the complexity of managing multiple properties or dealing with distant investments often makes professional management the more practical choice. By ensuring smooth operations, compliance with laws, and effective tenant management, a good property manager not only saves you time and stress but can also enhance the profitability and longevity of your real estate investments.

Bookkeeper/CPA

When diving into real estate investment, managing finances and ensuring compliance with tax regulations are as crucial as any other aspect of the business. Like referees in a sports game, the IRS ensures everyone plays by the rules, and failing to comply can lead to significant penalties. This is where a skilled bookkeeper or Certified Public Accountant (CPA) becomes indispensable to your team.

Taxes!

Navigating the tax maze is like reading an opposing team's defense in football — it requires careful analysis, strategic planning, and the ability to make quick adjustments to avoid costly missteps and capitalize on opportunities. Real estate investment brings numerous tax implications, from deductions for depreciation to the treatment of rental income and capital gains. The tax code is complex and frequently changing, posing a challenge for even the most savvy investors. A CPA who specializes in real estate can provide invaluable guidance, helping you to strategize effectively and maximize your tax benefits while staying within the bounds of the law.

One primary benefit of having a dedicated CPA or bookkeeper is their ability to navigate the intricacies of real estate taxation. They can advise on the best practices for structuring acquisitions, maximizing deductible expenses, and planning for taxes on sale profits. They will also be adept at handling more nuanced issues, such as the implications of the 1031 exchange—a tactic that allows investors to defer paying capital gains taxes on a property if it is sold and the proceeds are reinvested in a similar property.

Keeping Your Finances in Order

A professional bookkeeper or CPA does more than just prepare your tax returns; they manage your financial books throughout the year, ensuring that all financial transactions are accurately recorded. This meticulous record-keeping is essential not only for tax purposes but also for tracking the performance of your investments. You must know your stats! By maintaining clear and precise financial records, they help you assess which of your properties are most profitable and identify areas where costs can be reduced.

Moreover, a skilled CPA can assist in budgeting and financial forecasting, providing you with a clearer picture of your cash flow and helping you make informed decisions about future investments or potential sales. They can also guide you on financial risk management, ensuring you are not over-leveraged and that your investment strategy aligns with your overall financial goals.

Legal Compliance and Audits

The fear of an IRS audit is prominent in the minds of many investors. Having a CPA ensures that you are well-prepared should an audit occur. They can represent you before the IRS, providing detailed explanations for deductions and credits claimed and helping to navigate any issues that arise. This representation can be invaluable, potentially saving you from costly penalties and legal troubles.

Additionally, CPAs can keep you updated on current tax laws and upcoming changes that might affect your investment strategy. This proactive approach allows you to adjust your practices accordingly and take advantage of new tax benefits or avoid new pitfalls as legislation changes.

Choosing the Right CPA

Selecting the right CPA for your real estate investment business should be done with care. Look for a professional with extensive experience in real estate, as they will be most familiar with the specific financial and tax challenges you will face. They should not only be knowledgeable but also proactive, regularly offering you advice and updates on relevant financial matters.

It's also beneficial to choose a CPA who can communicate clearly and is available to answer your questions as they arise. The best CPAs are those who work as a strategic partner in your investment endeavors, not just as a service provider.

Incorporating a competent bookkeeper or CPA into your real estate investment team is crucial for maintaining financial health and legal compliance. They play a key role in ensuring that your investment operations run smoothly and are financially successful. By taking care of the financial intricacies of your investments, a good CPA allows you to focus more on the big-picture strategies that will grow your real estate portfolio.

Property Inspector

In the journey of real estate investing, the property inspector plays a pivotal role. Often referred to as a licensed home inspector, this professional provides an essential service by offering a detailed assessment of a property's condition. Their comprehensive reports are invaluable tools that guide investors in making informed decisions about purchases and renovations.

The Role of a Property Inspector

A property inspector conducts a thorough examination of a potential investment property, assessing everything from the foundation to the roof. This inspection covers major systems like plumbing, electrical, HVAC, and structural components of the building. The inspector's report provides a snapshot of the property's condition, highlighting any issues that need immediate attention or could require significant investment in the future.

For investors, the value of this report lies in its ability to inform the negotiation process. Understanding the extent of necessary repairs or potential problems can significantly affect the offer price on a property. It also aids in planning for renovations, allowing you to budget more accurately for necessary repairs or upgrades before they become costly surprises.

Decision-Making Insights

One of the key benefits of a detailed inspection report is the guidance it offers regarding immediate and future maintenance needs. For instance, if an inspector notes that a roof may soon need replacement, you can use this information to negotiate a lower purchase price or decide to allocate funds for this expense in the near future. Similarly, understanding the severity of issues like drywall cracks can help determine if they are merely cosmetic or indicative of deeper structural problems, such as foundation issues.

Property inspectors often recommend when to bring in specialists for a more detailed evaluation. For example, if the initial inspection suggests potential issues with the foundation, a structural engineer might be called in to provide a more detailed assessment and recommend specific repairs. These recommendations are crucial for ensuring the property is a sound investment and helps avoid unexpected and costly repairs after purchase.

Choosing the Right Inspector

Selecting a knowledgeable and experienced property inspector is crucial. Your real estate agent can be a valuable resource in this process, as they likely have contacts with reputable inspectors they have worked with in the past. When choosing an inspector, consider their credentials, experience, and familiarity with local building codes and common issues in the area where you are investing.

It's also important to ensure that the inspector's reports are clear, detailed, and useful for your decision-making process. A good inspector will not only provide a comprehensive report but will also be available to discuss their findings and explain the implications of any issues they uncover.

The Importance of Regular Inspections

For ongoing investments, regular inspections can help monitor the property's condition and ensure that maintenance issues are addressed promptly before they escalate into more significant problems. These inspections can be especially important if you own rental properties, as they help ensure that the property remains safe and appealing for tenants, thereby maximizing your rental income and maintaining the value of your investment. A good property management company will have these regular inspections as part of their regular processes.

A property inspector is an indispensable ally in the realm of real estate investing. By providing detailed and accurate information about the physical condition of properties, they enable investors to make informed decisions, plan effectively for renovations, and negotiate better deals. Their insights can ultimately save you time and money, making them an essential part of any successful real estate investment strategy.

House Cleaning Team

A clean and well-maintained property not only attracts better tenants and guests but also preserves the value of your investment. In the dynamic world of real estate investment, particularly in rental and short-term lease markets, the role of a professional house cleaning team cannot be overstated. They ensure your properties are in pristine condition for new tenants or guests, which is essential for maintaining high occupancy rates and securing top dollar returns.

The Importance of Make-Ready Cleaning

After a property undergoes renovation or a tenant moves out, make-ready cleaning is essential. This type of deep cleaning goes beyond the basics—it's about preparing the property to make a stellar first impression. For long-term rentals, a spotlessly clean home can be the deciding factor for potential tenants choosing your property over another.

A thorough cleaning after renovations also helps highlight the quality of the work done, ensuring that prospective tenants or buyers appreciate the updates and care put into the property. This attention to detail can increase the perceived value and help you command a higher rental or sale price.

Cleaning Services for Short-Term Rentals

For investors who manage short-term rental properties, cleaning services are even more critical. The turnaround time between guests can be very short, and the expectation for cleanliness is high. Professional cleaners can ensure that your property is spotless, stocked, and ready for new guests on a tight schedule. This not only enhances guest experience but also reduces the stress and time commitment on your part.

If you manage short-term rentals and plan to take personal vacations, relying on a trusted cleaning team is indispensable. It allows your property to continue generating income even when you are not available to oversee the cleaning yourself. This kind of reliability is crucial for maintaining a positive reputation among guests and ensuring that operational standards do not slip.

Choosing a Cleaning Service

When selecting a cleaning service, consider the following factors:

- **Reliability and Flexibility:** The team should be able to accommodate the often unpredictable schedule of property turnovers, especially in the case of short-term rentals.
- **Attention to Detail:** Ensure the service is thorough and accustomed to the high standards required for rental properties. They should not just clean but also inspect the property for any damages or issues that need addressing.
- **Experience in Rentals:** Choose a service experienced with rental properties, as they will understand the nuances and expectations of cleaning rental spaces versus residential homes.
- **Good Reviews and References:** Check reviews and ask for references. A reputable cleaning service should have a track record of satisfied customers.

Long-Term Benefits

Regular and professional cleaning extends beyond aesthetics; it also helps in the long-term maintenance of the property. By regularly removing dirt and debris, you reduce wear and tear on surfaces and appliances, potentially saving money on maintenance and repairs in the long run. Additionally, professional cleaners can help identify potential issues before they become significant problems, such as mold growth or water leaks, which might go unnoticed otherwise.

Incorporating a professional house cleaning team into your real estate investment strategy is a smart move that can enhance tenant satisfaction, maintain property condition, and ensure operational efficiency, especially for those managing multiple properties or engaging in the short-term rental market. By ensuring that each property is impeccably clean and well-maintained, you not only safeguard your investment but also enhance its profitability and appeal in a competitive market.

Networking Groups

You may have noticed a common player in many of these categories: the networking group.

In every city of any size, there are likely some sort of networking opportunities for real estate investors. Networking groups play a pivotal role in the world of real estate investing. These groups bring together like-minded individuals who share a common interest in real estate, providing a platform for learning, sharing experiences, and forming strategic partnerships. Whether you are a novice just starting out or a seasoned investor looking to expand your portfolio, participating in networking groups can significantly enhance your investment strategy.

The Value of Real Estate Networking Groups

Knowledge Sharing: One of the primary benefits of networking groups is the wealth of knowledge shared among members. Experienced investors often provide insights into market trends, investment strategies, and lessons learned from their own experiences. This information can be invaluable, helping you avoid common pitfalls and make informed decisions.

Resource Pooling: Networking groups often consist of individuals with diverse skill sets and resources. By connecting with other members, you can access a broader range of expertise and opportunities. For example, you might meet someone who specializes in property management, another who excels at finding undervalued properties, or someone else who has access to capital for new ventures. Together, you can leverage these resources to pursue opportunities that might be beyond your reach individually.

Investment Opportunities: Networking often leads to direct investment opportunities. Members of these groups frequently share leads on properties that are not yet on the market or that are being sold off-market at potentially lower prices. Additionally, partnerships formed within networking groups can lead to joint ventures or syndicated investments, allowing members to participate in larger deals.

Support and Mentorship: Real estate investing can be a complex and challenging field, especially for those who are new to it. Networking groups provide a support system where members can seek advice and mentorship from more experienced investors. This support can be indispensable in navigating the early stages of your investment career.

Finding the Right Networking Group

To derive the maximum benefit from networking groups, it's essential to find the right fit for your investment style and goals. Consider the following when choosing a group:

Focus and Specialty: Some networking groups might focus specifically on certain types of real estate, such as commercial properties, residential rentals, or flips. Others might cater to a particular aspect of investing, such as financing or development. Choose a group that aligns with your areas of interest and your investment strategy.

Location: While online networking groups offer broad access to resources and knowledge, local groups provide specific insights into the real estate market in your area. These groups can offer more relevant advice, especially on market conditions, local regulations, and networking opportunities with local professionals like real estate agents, contractors, and attorneys.

Size and Composition: The size of the group and the makeup of its membership can influence your experience. A smaller group might offer more personalized interaction and deeper relationships, while a larger group could provide a wider range of perspectives and opportunities. Consider what you are looking to gain from the group when deciding on the size.

Reputation and Reviews: Before joining a group, research its reputation. Look for reviews or testimonials from current or past members to gauge the group's effectiveness and the value it has provided to its members.

Making the Most of Networking Groups

To maximize the benefits of joining a networking group, be proactive. Attend meetings regularly, participate in discussions, volunteer for committees or speaking opportunities, and be willing to share your own experiences and resources. The more you engage with the group, the more you will benefit from it.

Networking is not just about taking; it's about giving back. By supporting other members, you build relationships and establish a reputation as a knowledgeable and reliable investor. These relationships can be the foundation of your future success in real estate investing.

Networking groups are more than just a gathering of professionals—they are dynamic leagues that can propel your real estate investment career forward. By joining the right group and actively participating, you can expand your knowledge, discover new opportunities, and build lasting relationships that will support and enhance your investment endeavors.

Conclusion

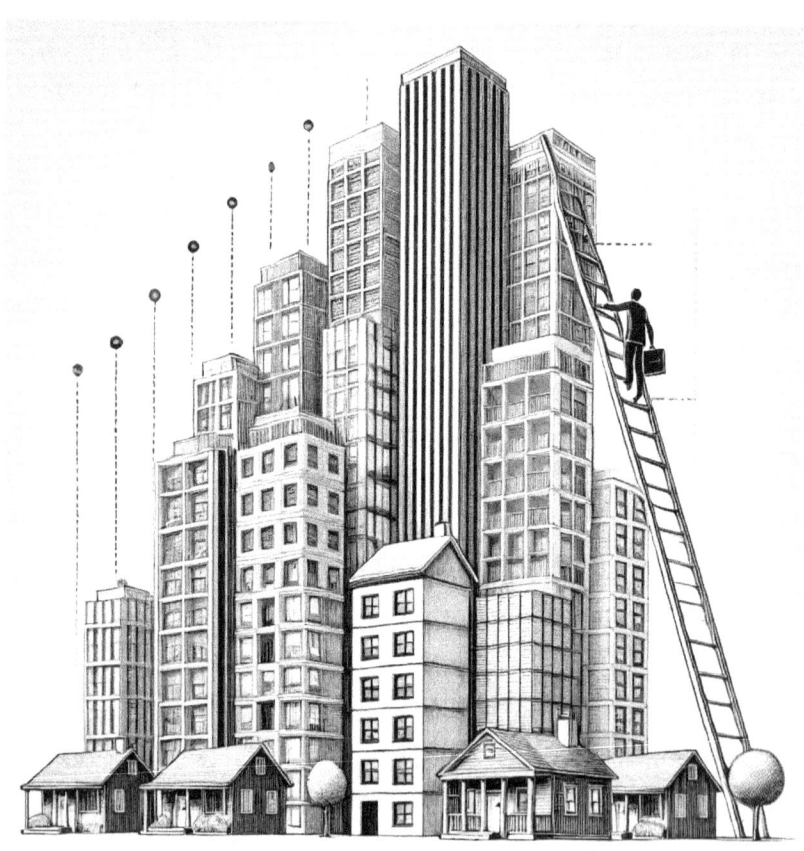

CONCLUSION

In the dynamic and competitive field of real estate investing, success is much like a well-coordinated team sport. Each player must excel in their role, from the scouts and coaches to the players on the field—each contributes to the overall victory. Throughout this book, we have likened the various aspects of real estate investing to building and refining a championship sports team, emphasizing the importance of strategy, teamwork, and diligence.

Building a Championship Team

Assembling Your Team: Just as a sports team relies on the collective strengths of its players, successful real estate investing depends on a diverse and skilled team. This team includes real estate agents, contractors, property managers, insurance agents, and more. Selecting the right team members is crucial—they must not only be skilled in their respective areas but also share a commitment to achieving your investment goals.

Strategic Playmaking: Every successful sports team needs a solid game plan, and the same goes for real estate investing. Developing a strategy that accounts for market conditions, financial analysis, and long-term goals is like a coach's playbook. It requires understanding the terrain, predicting opponents' moves, and adapting strategies as the game unfolds. Your investments should be similarly strategic, designed to maximize returns while managing risks.

Continuous Training and Adaptation: Top athletes spend countless hours training and improving their skills; similarly, real estate investors must commit to continuous learning and adaptation. The market is always changing, and staying informed through networking groups, ongoing education, and industry news is crucial. This knowledge allows you to pivot when necessary, much like a team adjusts its strategy at halftime based on the game's progress.

Playing to Win: In sports, the ultimate goal is to win championships. In real estate investing, the objective is to achieve financial success and build lasting wealth. This requires not only hard work and dedication but also the ability to execute your strategies effectively. It involves meticulous planning, precise execution, and the agility to manage and adapt to new challenges and opportunities as they arise.

Lessons from the Field

Teamwork is Essential: No single player wins the game. Real estate investing is a collaborative endeavor where success often hinges on the ability to work effectively with others, leveraging each team member's expertise to avoid pitfalls and capitalize on opportunities.

Preparation Meets Opportunity: Just as athletes must be ready to seize opportunities during a game, investors must be prepared to act when the right deal comes along. This readiness comes from thorough market research, financial preparedness, and the strategic foresight developed through experience and continuous learning.

Resilience is Key: In sports, teams often face setbacks and losses, but the best come back stronger. Real estate investors must similarly be resilient, learning from failures and persisting despite challenges. The market can be unforgiving, but with resilience, a clear strategy, and a strong team, you can navigate difficulties and emerge successful.

Wrapping Up

As we conclude this guide to real estate investing, remember that like any team sport, the key to success is a combination of strong leadership, strategic thinking, skilled execution, and continuous improvement. Whether you're just starting out or looking to expand your portfolio, the principles outlined in this book provide a foundation for building a robust investment strategy that can withstand the challenges and capitalize on the opportunities of the real estate market.

Embrace the spirit of teamwork, the dedication to training, and the strategic playmaking that define both champions on the field and successful investors in the real estate market. With these approaches, you're well on your way to securing your financial future and achieving your investment goals.

Resources

OpenAI. Year. "ChatGPT – Version 4o mini." Accessed August 20, 2024. https://www.openai.com/chatgpt

www.ingramcontent.com/pod-product-compliance
Lightning Source LLC
Chambersburg PA
CBHW070418230526
45471CB00006B/2875